THE WONDER OF SAFARI ANIMALS

THE WONDER OF SAFARI ANIMALS

FOG CITY PRESS

Published by Fog City Press,
a division of Weldon Owen Inc.
1045 Sansome Street
San Francisco, CA 94111 USA

www.weldonowen.com

weldon**owen**

President & Publisher Roger Shaw

Associate Publisher Mariah Bear

SVP, Sales & Marketing Amy Kaneko

Finance Manager Philip Paulick

Editor Bridget Fitzgerald

Creative Director Kelly Booth

Art Director Meghan Hildebrand

Senior Production Designer Rachel Lopez Metzger

Production Director Chris Hemesath

Associate Production Director Michelle Duggan

Director of Enterprise Systems Shawn Macey

Imaging Manager Don Hill

Library of Congress Control Number on file with the publisher.

ISBN 13: 978-1-68188-093-8
ISBN 10: 1-68188-093-8

10 9 8 7 6 5 4 3 2 1

2016 2017 2018 2019

Printed by 1010 Printing in China.

What are safari animals?
A safari is a journey, and safari
animals are creatures that
are so special, they're worth
taking a trip to just see them.

The animals you'll find in this
book are from Africa, and
for many of us, Africa is very
far away. But by turning the
page, you can start your own
safari—a journey where you'll
meet some amazing animals!

On the plains of Africa, animals will often travel in groups. A group of hippos is called a bloat or a pod.

Hippopotamus

African Lion Cub

Fun Fact

A group of zebras is called a herd or a zeal!

Zebra

Fun Fact

Female African fish eagles are larger than males.

White Rhinoceros

Blesbok

Sometimes, you find animals on their own, but they mostly stick together for safety.

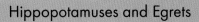

Fun Fact

Birds help to keep the hippos' skin clean by eating bugs.

Impala

Animals often hang out with their own kind.
But sometimes, very different creatures
team up, like hippos and birds.

Meerkat

Young animals learn from the other members of their families, just like we do.

Guinea Fowl

Hippopotamus

Fun Fact

Warthogs can smell food beneath the ground.

Puku

Baby animals usually stay close to their mothers.

African Elephant

African Lion Cub

Fun Fact

Elephants can communicate using touch and smell.

African Elephant

Puku

. . . like jumping, flying, and roaring!

Secretary Bird

Fun Fact

You can hear a lion roar from five miles away!

Fun Fact

Cranes have been
around for over
38 million years!

Secretary Bird

Bateleur Eagle

Africa is home to many amazing birds. Some have feathers that look like fancy hats!

Safari animals hunt in different ways: some use sharp teeth, some squeeze with a tight grip, and others grab with strong claws.

Martial Eagle

Rock Python

Serval

Fun Fact

Vervets spend hours grooming each other.

Chacma Baboon

With teeth like these, it's hard to believe this monkey eats mostly fruit!

Fun Fact

Caracals hunt
rodents, birds,
and small deer.

African Wild Dog

Animals that eat meat—like caracals, wild dogs, and hyenas—have strong teeth and jaws. The better to bite with!

Brown Hyena

Gazelle

Other safari animals are gentle plant eaters, happiest when they have some tasty grass or berries to munch.

Blue Duiker

Fun Fact

Waterbucks can grow to 500 pounds (227 kg)!

Defassa Waterbuck

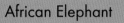
African Elephant

Fun Fact

Elephants are the largest land-living mammals on Earth.

Crested Grebe

Ground Squirrel

Sometimes even crunchy bugs are on the menu. Animal meals are as different as the creatures eating them.

Fun Fact

Galagos are also called "bush babies."

Galago

Some animals have large ears so they can hear the things going on around them.

Leopard

These animals have a great sense of sight, which is handy for hunting or getting around in the dark.

Galago

Fun Fact

Ospreys hunt for fish from high above, then dive!

Osprey

Fun Fact

The kudu's horns can be 72 inches (1.8 m) long!

Nyala

Other animals have great horns that they can use for wrestling or breaking off branches to reach leaves.

Red Hartebeest

Cheetah

Fun Fact

Cheetahs can run up to 75 miles per hour (120 kph)!

Hunters and people moving into Africa's natural environments cause big problems for the animals.

Bontebok

Black-and-White Colobus

Fun Fact

A grown elephant is too big for most predators.

African Elephant

Fun Fact

Gorillas can eat
66 pounds (30 kg)
of food each day!

Nile Monitor Lizard

Warthog

Some animals that were once common across Africa now live in only a handful of places.

Fun Fact

Many groups help to save endangered animals.

Giraffe

But if people work together, we can keep these wonderful animals in our world for a long, long time!

Flamingo